# Tell Me Why

# WHY?

## My Fingernails Grow

Samantha Bell

Published in the United States of America by Cherry Lake Publishing
Ann Arbor, Michigan
www.cherrylakepublishing.com

Content Adviser: Charisse Gencyuz, M.D., Clinical Instructor, Department of Internal Medicine,
University of Michigan
Reading Adviser: Marla Conn, ReadAbility, Inc.

Photo Credits: © bonzodog/Shutterstock Images, cover, 1, 5; © Samuel Borges Photography/Shutterstock
Images, cover, 1, 15; © rmnoa357/Shutterstock Images, cover, 1, 9; © Matt Jeppson /Shutterstock Images,
cover, 1, 5; © ponsulak/Shutterstock Images, cover, 1, 15; © View Factor Images/Shutterstock Images,
cover, 1, 13; © michaeljung/Shutterstock Images, back cover; © JPC-PROD/Shutterstock Images, 7;
Dorling Kindersley/Thinkstock, 9; © Blend Images/Shutterstock Images, 11; © karelnoppe/Shutterstock
Images, 17; © olmarmar/Shutterstock Images, 21

Library of Congress Cataloging-in-Publication Data

Bell, Samantha, author.
  My fingernails grow / by Samantha Bell.
      pages cm. -- (Tell me why)
  Summary: "Offers answers to questions about our nails and the protein
keratin. Explanations and appealing photos encourage readers to continue
their quest for knowledge. Text features and search tools, including a
glossary and an index, help students locate information and learn new
words."-- Provided by publisher.
  Audience: K to grade 3.
  Includes bibliographical references and index.
  ISBN 978-1-63188-009-4 (hardcover) -- ISBN 978-1-63188-052-0 (pbk.) --
ISBN 978-1-63188-095-7 (pdf) -- ISBN 978-1-63188-138-1 (ebook)  1.
Fingernails--Juvenile literature. 2.  Keratin--Juvenile literature.  I.
Title.

  QM488.B45 2015
  612--dc23

                              2014005661

Cherry Lake Publishing would like to acknowledge the work of The Partnership for 21st Century Skills.
Please visit www.p21.org for more information.

Printed in the United States of America
Corporate Graphics Inc.

# Table of Contents

# Many Important Jobs

Max loves to be outside. He makes forts and digs in the garden. But he does not like getting dirt under his fingernails. Sometimes it is hard to clean them.

It is important for Max to take care of his fingernails. They help keep the fingertips safe. They make it easier to pick up small things. They help scratch an itch.

It is easy for dirt to get under fingernails.
Nails need to be kept clean.

Fingernails have another job, too. They can tell a doctor if someone is sick. The doctor looks at the fingernails and might press on them. If a person's fingernails are unhealthy, the body is probably unhealthy, too.

When Max comes inside, he washes his hands. He also has to scrub his fingernails. Sometimes he must clip them, too. Then they are shorter and easier to clean.

Soon he will have to clip them again. Max frowns. Why do his fingernails keep growing, anyway?

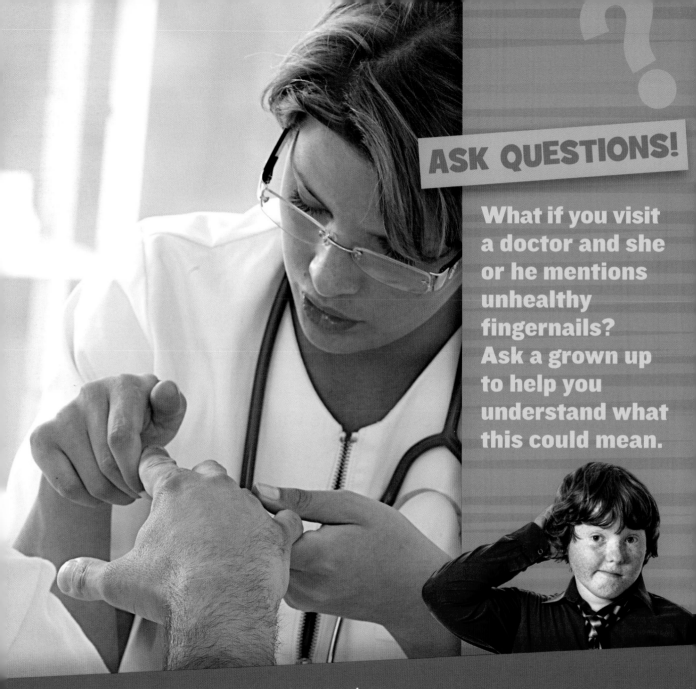

What if you visit a doctor and she or he mentions unhealthy fingernails? Ask a grown up to help you understand what this could mean.

*A doctor might check your fingernails for signs of health problems.*

# From the Beginning

People have fingernails even before they are born. A baby's fingernails are very tiny. But they are just like a grown-up's nails. All fingernails are made of the same **protein**. This protein is called **keratin**. Keratin is also found in hair and skin.

Fingernails have different parts. The nail plate is the largest part. The **lunula** is near the bottom of the nail. This is the white part that looks like a half-moon. The **cuticle** overlaps the lunula. Under the cuticle is the **matrix**.

Nail Matrix

Cuticle　Lunula

Nail Plate

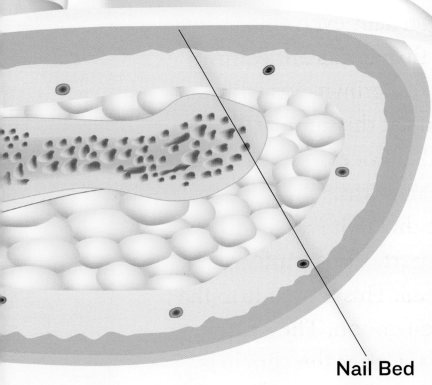

Nail Bed

*This diagram shows the parts of a fingernail.*
*A toenail has the same parts.*

## LOOK!

**Compare this drawing to your own fingernail. Can you see your nail plate and lunula?**

Healthy fingernails are smooth. They do not have spots or marks. Unhealthy fingernails have dents or lines. Sometimes they are strange colors.

Many fingernails have **ridges**. As a person gets older, the ridges are easier to see. Some ridges go from the tip of the nail to the cuticle. These fingernails are healthy. Some ridges go across from one side to the other. This means that something is wrong.

*Healthy fingernails all look the same.*

# Right-Handed or Left-Handed?

The body is made of **cells**. Fingernails are made of cells, too. New cells are always being made. The new cells make Max's fingernails grow.

Fingernails seem to grow from the tips. But they actually grow from under the cuticle. New fingernail cells are made in the matrix. The keratin in the old cells makes them flat and hard. The old cells are pushed out toward the fingertips.

*Children's fingernails grow faster than adults' fingernails.*

Fingernails grow about one-tenth of an inch (3 millimeters) each month. But sometimes they grow faster. Children's fingernails grow faster than those of adults. Warm weather can make fingernails grow faster, too. So does eating healthy food.

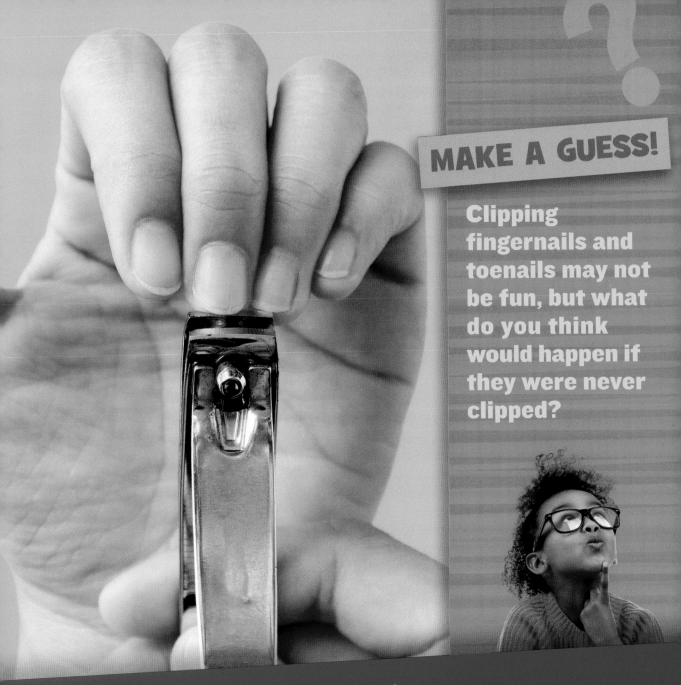

Clipping fingernails and toenails may not be fun, but what do you think would happen if they were never clipped?

*Fingernails need to be trimmed when they get too long.*

Fingernails grow at different rates on each hand. Some people are right-handed. The nails on the right hand grow faster. Other people are left-handed. The nails on the left hand grow faster. The thumb has the fastest-growing nail. The little finger has the slowest.

*Are you right-handed or left-handed?*
*Have you noticed a difference in how your nails grow?*

# Healthy Nails

Max does not like clipping his fingernails and toenails. Toenails don't grow as fast as fingernails. A whole fingernail can grow in about six months. A new toenail grows in about 12 to 18 months.

Max should keep his fingernails and toenails clean and dry. This helps keep **bacteria** from growing under them. His mom shows him how to clip a **hangnail**, too. It could be very painful if he pulls this piece of skin from the side of his fingernail.

*Toenails are made of keratin, just like fingernails.*

Max might have trouble with a fingernail sometimes. Many problems can be taken care of at home. Even some nail injuries are not hard to treat. But it can be more serious. Pain and redness might mean **infection**. Then Max's mom will call the doctor.

Max still does not like scrubbing his fingernails. But he is glad his fingernails are healthy and growing.

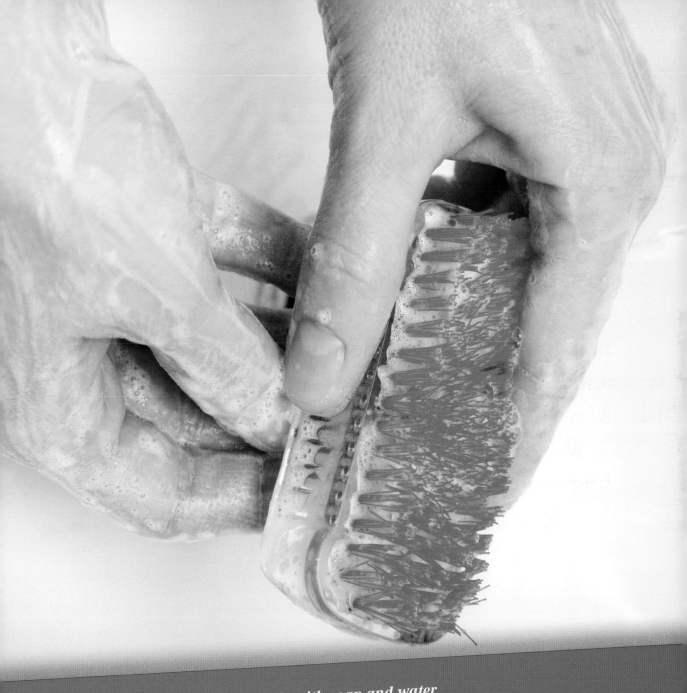

*Scrubbing fingernails and toenails with soap and water will help keep them clean and healthy.*

# Think About It

Are you able to tell if a fingernail is healthy or unhealthy? If you need a grown-up's help finding the answer, don't be afraid to ask.

Could you tell a friend the parts of a fingernail by looking at his or her fingers?

What else do you want to know about fingernails? Write a list of at least three questions. Then look for answers online or at the library.

# Glossary

**bacteria** (bak-TEER-ee-uh) microscopic organisms that can cause disease

**cells** (SELZ) tiny units that are the building blocks of all living things

**cuticle** (KYOO-ti-kuhl) the skin that overlaps the base of a fingernail

**hangnail** (HANG-neyl) a piece of torn skin on the side of a fingernail

**infection** (in-FEK-shuhn) when the body contains a disease or a harmful organism

**keratin** (KER-uh-tin) the protein found in hair, skin, and fingernails

**lunula** (LOO-nyuh-lee) the white part of the fingernail located at the base

**matrix** (MEY-triks) the part of the fingernail under the cuticle where new cells are made

**protein** (PROH-teen) substances in the body that are necessary for life and found in different foods

**ridges** (RIJ-ehz) narrow, raised strips on the surface of something

# Find Out More

### Books:

Amsel, Sheri. *The Everything Kids' Human Body Book: All You Need to Know About Your Body Systems—From Head to Toe!* Avon, MA: Adams Media Corp., 2012.

Schaefer, Lola M. *Arms, Elbows, Hands, and Fingers.* Chicago: Heinemann Library, 2003.

Smith, Penny, ed. *Human Body Encyclopedia.* New York: DK Publishing, 2005.

### Web Site:

KidsHealth—Your Nails
*http://kidshealth.org/kid/htbw/your_nails.html*
Learn more about common nail problems and nail care.

# Index

## About the Author

Samantha Bell is a children's writer and illustrator living in South Carolina with her husband, four children, and lots of animals. She has illustrated a number of picture books, including some of her own. She has also written magazine articles, stories, and poems, as well as craft, activity, and wildlife books. She loves animals, being outdoors, and learning about all the amazing wonders of nature.